TO: _____

FROM: _____

THE JOY OF THE LORD IS YOUR STRENGTH.

—Nehemiah 8:10

ZondervanPublishingHouse

Mail Drop B20
Grand Rapids, Michigan 49530
http://www.zondervan.com

Editorial Director: Joy Marple
Project Editor: Robin Schmitt
Production Editor: Pat Matuszak
Art Director: Robin Welsh
Designer: Christopher Tobias/Tobias Design
Photographer: Dennis Frates/Oregon Scenics

Printed in China
97 98 99 /HK/ 3 2 1

DISCOVERING

joy

Photography by Dennis Frates

ZondervanGifts

We have a gift for inspiration™

joy

You have made known to me the path of life; you will

fill me with joy in your presence, with eternal pleasures

at your right hand.

—Psalm 16:11

Isaac went out to the field one evening to meditate. —Genesis 24:63

People living in cities today would do well to follow the example of Isaac and as often as possible visit the fields of the countryside, away from the hustle and bustle of the city.… *A walk through a field, a stroll by a seashore, or a hike across a meadow sprinkled with daisies will purge you of the impurities of life and will cause your heart to beat with new joy and hope.*

Have you ever risen early, climbed a hill, and watched God make a morning? The dull gray gives way as he pushes the sun toward the horizon, and then the tints and hues of every color begin to blend into one perfect light as the full sun suddenly bursts into view. As king of the day, the sun moves majestically across the sky, flooding the earth and every deep valley with glorious light. At this point, you can hear the music of heaven's choir as it sings of the majesty of God himself and of the glory of the morning.

joy

WHERE MORNING DAWNS AND EVENING FADES

YOU CALL FORTH SONGS OF JOY.

—Psalm 65:8

All my springs of joy are in you, O God. —Psalm 87:7 NASB

If I see God in everything, he will calm and color everything I see! Perhaps the circumstances causing my sorrows will not be removed and my situation will remain the same, but if Christ is brought into my grief and gloom as my Lord and Master, he will "surround me with songs of deliverance" (Psalm 32:7).

—Hannah Whitall Smith

God is in every tomorrow,

Therefore I live for today,

Certain of finding at sunrise,

Guidance and strength for my way;

Power for each moment of weakness,

Hope for each moment of pain,

Comfort for every sorrow,

Sunshine and joy after rain.

THANKS BE TO GOD, WHO ALWAYS LEADS US
IN TRIUMPHAL PROCESSION IN CHRIST.

—2 Corinthians 2:14

Rejoice in the Lord always.

I will say it again: Rejoice! —Philippians 4:4

I still believe that a day of understanding will come for each of us, however far away it may be. *We will understand as we see the tragedies that today darken and dampen the presence of heaven for us take their proper place in God's great plan—a plan so overwhelming, magnificent, and joyful, we will laugh with wonder and delight.*

—Arthur Christopher Bacon

Oh, let us rejoice in the Lord, evermore,

When darts of the Tempter are flying,

For Satan still dreads, as he oft did before,

Our singing much more than our sighing.

Be filled with the Spirit.... Sing and make music in

your heart to the Lord.

—Ephesians 5:18–19

The LORD is my strength and my shield; my heart trusts in him,

and I am helped. My heart leaps for joy and I will give thanks to him in song.

—Psalm 28:7

It is said that springs of sweet, fresh water pool up amid the saltiness of the oceans, that the fairest Alpine flowers bloom in the wildest and most rugged mountain passes, and that the most magnificent psalms arose from the most profound agonies of the soul. *May it continue to be!* Therefore, amid a multitude of trials, souls who love God will discover reasons for boundless, leaping joy.

—from *Tried as by Fire*

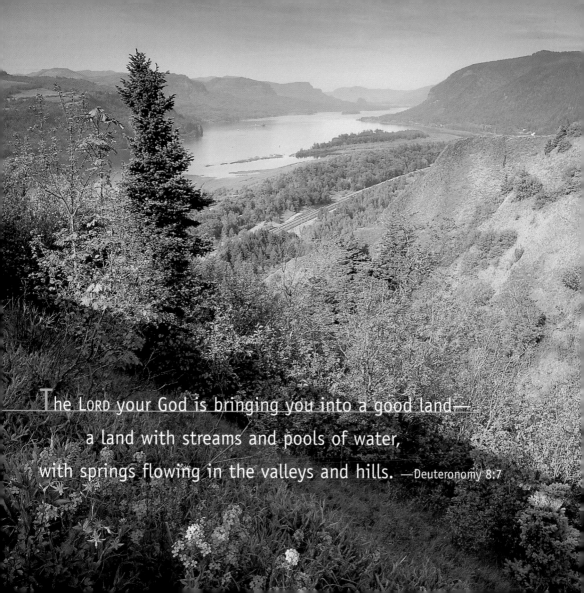

The LORD your God is bringing you into a good land—
a land with streams and pools of water,
with springs flowing in the valleys and hills. —Deuteronomy 8:7

THE EAGLE THAT SOARS AT GREAT ALTITUDES

DOES NOT WORRY ABOUT HOW IT WILL CROSS A RIVER.

It is easier to sing your worries away than to reason them away.

Why not sing in the morning? Think of the birds—they are the first

to sing each day, and they have fewer worries than anything else in

creation. And don't forget to sing in the evening, which is what the

robins do when they have finished their daily work. Once they have

flown their last flight of the day and gathered the last bit of food,

they find a treetop from which to sing a song of praise.

This is exactly how God deals with every child of his when we truly sacrifice. *We surrender everything we own and accept poverty—then he sends wealth....We surrender all our cherished hopes* and die to self—then he sends overflowing joy.

—Dr. C. G. Trumbull

Put your hope in God, for I will yet praise him. —Psalm 42:5

The Lord is sure to accomplish those things,

O trusting heart, the Lord to you has told;

Let faith and hope arise, and lift their wings,

To soar toward the sunrise clouds of gold;

The doorways of the rosy dawn swing wide,

Revealing joys the darkness of night did hide.

—Bessie Porter

WHEN THE LORD CALLS YOU TO COME ACROSS THE WATER,

STEP OUT WITH CONFIDENCE AND JOY. AND NEVER

GLANCE AWAY FROM HIM FOR EVEN A MOMENT.

I have learned to love the darkness of sorrow,

for it is there I see the brightness of God's face. —Madame Guyon

Nothing that is not part of God's will is allowed to

come into the life of someone who trusts and obeys

him. *This truth should be enough to make our life one of*

ceaseless thanksgiving and joy, because God's will is the

most hopeful, pleasant, and glorious thing in the world.

—H. W. S.

If I experience the presence of God in his majesty through my pain and loss, so that I bow before him and pray,

"Your will be done" (Matthew 6:10),

then I have gained much indeed. God gave Job glimpses of his future glory, for in those weary and difficult days and nights, he was allowed to penetrate God's veil and could honestly say,

"I know that my Redeemer lives" (Job 19:25).

—from *In the Hour of Silence*

THEN JOB REPLIED TO THE LORD:

"I KNOW THAT YOU CAN DO ALL THINGS;

NO PLAN OF YOURS CAN BE THWARTED."

—Job 42:1-2

"Until now you have not asked for anything in my name. Ask and you will receive, and your joy will be complete." —John 16:

I like to cultivate the spirit of happiness! *It retunes my soul and keeps it so perfectly in tune that Satan is afraid to touch it.* The chords of my soul become so vibrant and full of heavenly electricity that he takes his fiendish fingers from me and goes somewhere else! *Satan is always wary of interfering with me when my heart is full of the happiness and joy of the Holy Spirit.*

ARE YOU EXPERIENCING SORROW? PRAYER CAN MAKE YOUR TIME
OF AFFLICTION ONE OF STRENGTH AND SWEETNESS.
ARE YOU EXPERIENCING HAPPINESS? PRAYER CAN ADD A HEAVENLY
FRAGRANCE TO YOUR TIME OF JOY.
—Farrar

Holiness appears to me to have a sweet, calm, pleasant, charming, and serene nature, all of which brings an inexpressible purity, radiance, peacefulness, and overwhelming joy to the soul. In other words, holiness makes the soul like a field or garden of God, with every kind of pleasant fruit and flower, and each one delightful and undisturbed, enjoying a sweet calm and the gentle and refreshing rays of the sun.

—Jonathan Edwards

We always enjoy looking down a long road lined with beautiful trees. *The trees are a delightful sight and seem to be forming a temple of plants, with strong wooden pillars and arches of leaves.* In the same way you look down a beautiful road like this, why not look back on the road of the years of your life? *Look at the large green limbs of God's mercy overhead and the strong pillars of his loving-kindness and faithfulness that have brought you much joy.* Do you see any birds singing in the branches? If you look closely, surely you will see many, for they are singing of God's mercy received "thus far."

—Charles H. Spurgeon

With singing lips my mouth will praise you, O God. —Psalm 63:5

joy

BE LIKE A BIRD THAT, HALTING IN ITS

FLIGHT, RESTS ON A LIMB TOO SLIGHT.

AND FEELING IT GIVE WAY BENEATH HIM SINGS,

KNOWING HE HAS WINGS.

Do you believe that your heavenly Father will let you carry the banner of his victory and joy to the very front of the battle, only to calmly withdraw to see you captured or beaten back by the enemy? Never! His Holy Spirit will sustain you in your bold advance and fill your heart with gladness and praise.

Not a single blow can hit,

Till the God of love sees fit.

Do not be afraid to enter the cloud descending on your life, for God is in it. *And the other side is radiant with his glory.* "Do not be surprised at the painful trial you are suffering, as though something strange were happening to you. *But rejoice that you participate in the sufferings of Christ*" (1 Peter 4:12–13). When you feel the most forsaken and lonely, God is near. *He is in the darkest cloud.* Forge ahead into the darkness without flinching, knowing that under the shelter of the cloud, God is waiting for you.

He who dwells in the shelter of the Most High

will rest in the shadow of the Almighty. —Psalm 91:1

Isn't there something captivating about the sight of a person burdened with many trials, yet who is as lighthearted as the sound of a bell? Isn't there something contagious and valiant in seeing others who are greatly tempted but are "more than conquerors" (Romans 8:37)? Isn't it heartening to see a fellow traveler whose body is broken, yet who retains the splendor of unbroken patience? What a witness these give to the power of God's gift of grace!

—Dr. J. H. Jowett

IN THE HOLY HUSH OF THE EARLY DAWN
I HEAR A VOICE—
"I AM WITH YOU ALL THE DAY,
REJOICE! REJOICE!"

Sing to the Lord, always giving thanks to God the Father for everything. —Ephesians 5:19-20

It is not difficult for the Lord to turn night into day.

He who sends the clouds can just as easily clear the skies.

Let us be encouraged—things are better down the road.

Let us sing God's praises in anticipation of things to come.

—Charles H. Spurgeon

I had recently received bad news from home, and deep shadows of darkness seemed to cover my soul. I prayed but the darkness remained. I forced myself to endure but the shadows only deepened. Then suddenly one day, as I entered a missionary's home at an inland station, I saw these words on the wall: "Try giving thanks." So I did, and in a moment every shadow was gone, never to return. Yes, the psalmist was right: "It is good to praise the LORD" (Psalm 92:1).

—Rev. Henry W. Frost

FOR YOU MAKE ME GLAD BY YOUR DEEDS, O LORD;

I SING FOR JOY AT THE WORKS OF YOUR HANDS.

—Psalm 92:4

WAIT AT GOD'S PROMISE UNTIL HE MEETS YOU THERE,
FOR HE ALWAYS RETURNS BY THE PATH OF HIS PROMISES.

Begin the day with God! He is your Sun and Day!

His is the radiance of your dawn; To him address your day.

Sing a new song at morn! Join the glad woods and hills;

Join the fresh winds and seas and plains, Join the bright flowers and rills.

Sing your first song to God! Not to your fellow men;

Not to the creatures of his hand, But to the glorious one.

Take your first walk with God! Let him go forth with thee;

By stream, or sea, or mountain path, Seek still his company.

Your first transaction be, With God himself above;

So will your business prosper well, All the day be love.

—Horatius Bonar

JESUS CHRIST IS NOT MY SECURITY
AGAINST THE STORMS OF LIFE,
BUT HE IS MY PERFECT SECURITY IN THE STORMS.
HE HAS NEVER PROMISED ME AN EASY PASSAGE,
ONLY A SAFE LANDING.